Origami: Rokoan Style #2

The Art of Connecting Cranes

by Masako Sakai & Michie Sahara

Heian

© 2001 Masako Sakai and Michie Sahara
Edited by: Dianne Ooka
Photographed by: Don Farber
Diagram Illustration and Typography: Ashley B. Lang

First Edition 2001
01 02 03 04 05 10 9 8 7 6 5 4 3 2 1

ISBN: 0-89346-932-7

Heian International, Inc.
1815 W. 205th Street, Suite #301
Torrance, CA 90501
E-mail: Heianemail@heian.com
Website: www.heian.com

Printed in Singapore

Table of Contents

Part 1:

In this volume...

How to fold an Origami Crane, the traditional way
Origami Crane...the quick and easy way
Basic folds and symbols

Part 2:

Instructions for models created by Rokoan

Part 3:

More on presentation
Using finishing Origami works as interior decorations

Part 1:

In this volume...
More Rokoan Style Origami

In, *Origami: Rokoan Style*, we introduced the Buddhist priest Rokoan Gido (1761 – 1834) and his unique origami style. His book, *Senbatsuru Orikata* (1797) which is considered to be the oldest book on origami, featured 49 different models of his designs. We introduced 25 of his models and one of co-author Masako Sakai's creations in our previous book. Here we introduce the rest of the models and again one of Masako Sakai's originals. The first 25 models were all progressively challenging and consisted of varied designs. The 24 models presented here are again unique and interesting and even more challenging. #43 Hyakutsuru (One Hundred Cranes) and #50 Karyobin (Phoenix) are the most challenging. #43 Hyakutsuru requires much patience, while #50 Karyobin requires both precise technique and patience. Many models use the Blintz Fold which requires thin and strong washi papers like Chiri-zome, Itajime and Mino-gami. There aren't very many models where Yuzenshi can be used. Determine the best type of paper for each model from the photographs of our examples.

The sequence of models in this second volume is much different from Rokoan's original book. We have rearranged his sequence according to our teaching experience. Our students have always been eager to fold #43 Hyakutsuru; therefore, when teaching, we decided to conclude with this model. We have chosen models that are different and interesting up to #43 Hyakutsuru. The models after #43 are made up of similar patterns with various results except for #50 Karyobin. #50 Karyobin is difficult to fold; we could not find suitable paper until we tried Chiri-zome. Mino-gami was too expensive. Chiri-zome is thin but also has body. It is perfect for #50 Karyobin with its many layers of paper. Consequently, when we finished teaching #43 Hyakutsuru, our students wanted to continue and finish all the models created by Rokoan. Chiri-zome enabled us to teach all the models by Rokoan.

Since the drawings in the original book by Rokoan were not clear, a number of origamists through history interpreted the folds differently. The instructions in this book are our own interpretation; the same model may be folded differently, but the end results are usually the same.

Even in Japan where Rokoan created this origami style, there are not many origamists who have re-created all of the models. If you found that the models in our previous book, *Origami: Rokoan Style*, were difficult, you will find that the models in this book are even more challenging. We hope you will enjoy folding all of them. Once you're done, you might wish to design your own. Please try to have a purpose in mind and don't design simply to increase the number of cranes. Come up with a title and perhaps even an accompanying poem. Be creative and honor the original designer, Rokoan Gido.

How to fold an Origami Crane...
The traditional way

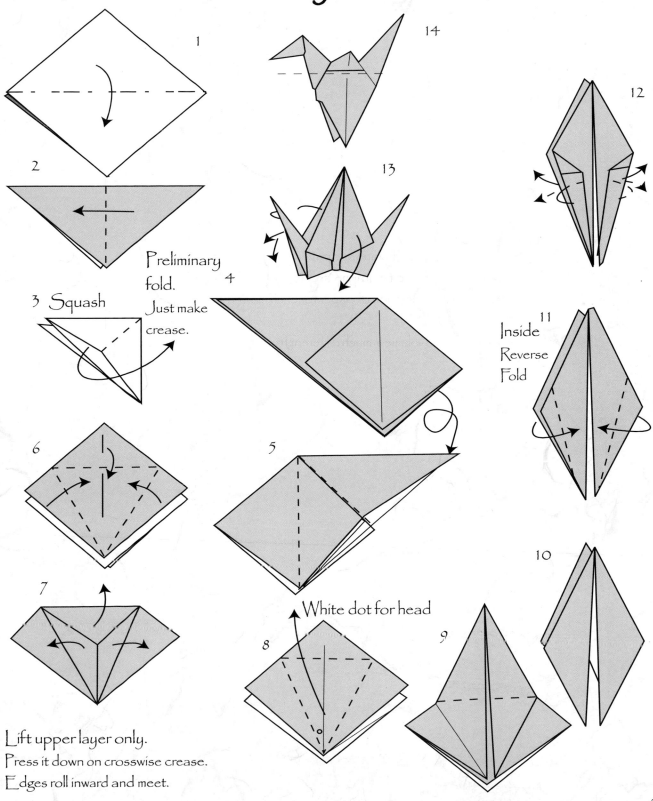

1

14

13

12

2

Preliminary fold.
Just make crease.

3 Squash

4

Inside Reverse Fold

11

6

5

7

10

White dot for head

8

9

Lift upper layer only.
Press it down on crosswise crease.
Edges roll inward and meet.

5

Origami Crane
The Quick and Easy Way

The traditional method of folding a crane is illustrated on the previous page. For Rokoan Style Origami, it is beneficial to know how to fold a crane as easily as possible since you are folding multiple cranes that are all connected at the head, tail and wings. Here is a short-cut that gets to step #10 of traditional crane folding very quickly.

1. Make a vertical crease, a horizontal crease and diagonal creases. All creases are Mountain Fold except for one of the diagonal creases (which is going to represent a head and a tail). This will be Valley Fold. Be sure to do the vertical and horizontal creases firmly as this will help you later when you want the back of the crane to go up when you do the move in #3.

2. Fold corner B to line A–C, making crease A-b. Fold corner D to line A–C, making crease A-d. Do the same for all corners. When folding multiple cranes, make these creases for all the cranes before starting to fold each crane. This might seem like more folding, but it is better in the long run. First, it gives more precise creases than the traditional #6 fold. Second, it is easier to get to #10 than folding the traditional folds #8 and #9.

Diagram for #1 and #2

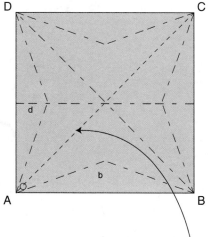

Diagram for #3

3. All corners (A through D) of the origami crane paper represent head, tail or wings. With the Rokoan Style Origami, the head is designated by marking it with a little white dot. Since A is marked as the head, C is the tail and B and D therefore are wings. Fold diagonal crease A–C as a Valley Fold and bring A to meet C.

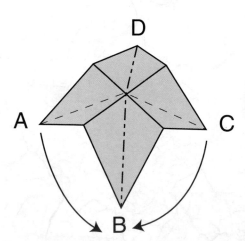

4. Lift wings B and D. Now you are at step #10 of the traditional crane fold.

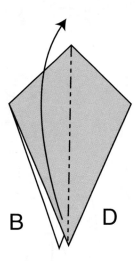

B   D   Diagram for #4

5. At step #11 of the traditional crane fold, you fold to the center. With our method, however, you fold about 2/3 of the way, leaving about 1/3 space from the center. This makes the head and tail neater. Since washi is thicker than regular origami paper, folding it in the traditional way makes the head look too bulky—like a dinosaur's head.

Leave about 1/3 space from center.

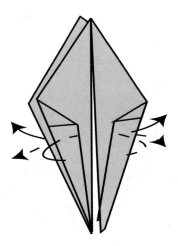

Diagram for #5

Tips for Rokoan Origami Style of Folding:

1. Regardless of which model you are folding, do not forget to make all the creases at the beginning before you fold an individual crane. Even a difficult model can be folded with ease when all the creases are made ahead.

2. Before you fold, mark each head with a white dot on the right side of your paper. When folding multiple numbers of cranes, marking heads is the only way for you to know where all the heads are. A black dot is used to mark a head that is to match another head with a white dot. This is done when two sheets of paper are folded to make one crane. Usually the right side of the paper marked with a black dot is placed under the wrong side of the paper with the white dot marked on its right side.

3. Remember that the head is where you make the Valley Fold. This means that the opposite of the head, the tail, is also done with the Valley Fold.

4. The connection between the cranes, which you leave uncut, is approximately 1/8".

5. Areas marked with triangles are unused portions. This area is to be included into a crane. Each instruction will tell you into which crane you should include it. Rokoan's original instruction states it this way. We feel you should be able to fold layers of Mingeishi, Ita-jime, Chiri-zome and Jo-washi, but it is very difficult to fold layers of Yuzen since it is thick with colorful paints. You should cut the area marked with a triangle (unused portion) in order to fold smoothly. In Rokoan's time it is believed that only white washi was available. So this was not a problem.

6. The models in this book should be completed in their sequence of presentation, since they become progressively difficult.

If you pay attention to the above points you can fold all models with ease.

Basic Folds and Symbols

Valley Fold

Mountain Fold

Existing Crease

Direction to Fold

Zabuton Ori **or**
Blintz Fold

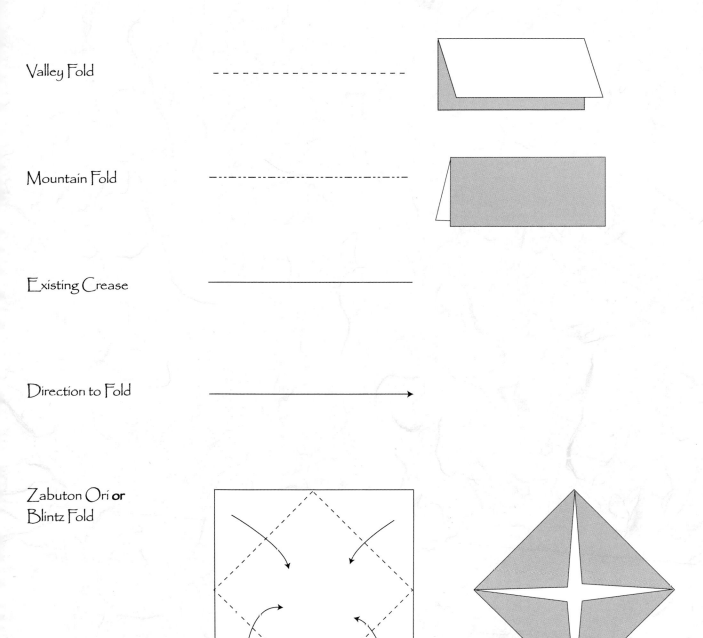

Shaded area is the right side of the paper.

Part 2

27. Mitsudomoe... Threesome

As in #20 Kanae, fold two pieces of squares marked with a triangle to make a circle. With this model, the degree of incision is less and hence more difficult to fold.

Note:

Two squares marked with triangles are folded together to make a circle. Please note that all the cuts to make four squares are one third of the total length except where two squares are to be folded together. There the cut is half of the total length. Be sure to fold in the order of A, B, and C, matching the two squares. As always, do not forget to make all the creases before folding. Since two pieces of paper are being folded together, fairly thin paper is recommended.

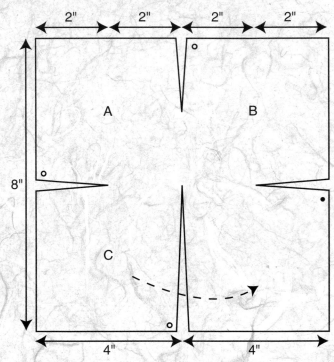

28. Yokogumo... Stratus Cloud

This refers to a cloud that floats sideways in the sky. Like its unique title, the design is very original and the folding method is interesting. Since the Blintz Fold is used to fold all the cranes, thin and strong washi must be used to create this model.

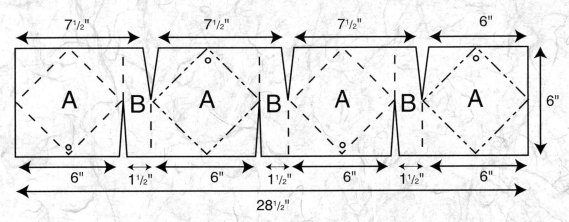

Note:

Cut as marked on the drawing. Make creases as marked with dotted lines on the drawing. Also, make creases diagonally, vertically and horizontally on each square as when folding a crane. Blintz fold each square, but fold one facing up, then turn it over and fold, then turn it back and fold, and turn it over again and fold. When folding blintz, the extra paper B is folded into each blintz marked A. Use a long hair pin or a large paper clip to keep blintzes in place.

Then proceed to fold each blintz into a crane. It is easier to fold if each blintz is lightly glued in place. Stick glue is best.

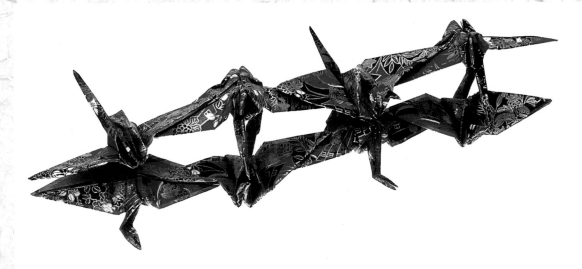

29. Haru no Akebono... The Dawn of Spring

This model uses the Blintz Fold again. Thin and strong washi is recommended. The pattern is very intricate and unique. Please study the drawing carefully before cutting and marking the crane heads.

Note:

The baby cranes are attached to the back of the adult crane's wings. This is a very difficult model to fold, and the possibility of tearing at the connections is great. Leave ample space at the connections—a little more than usual.

Start by folding the baby cranes first. Then blintz fold the large square, tacking the unused portion inside the blintz with a glue stick, and fold the adult crane.

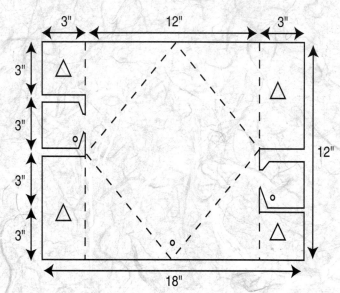

30. Furan... Orchid Rustling in the Wind

Here four baby cranes are attached to the adult crane under the wings. The unused portions of paper are folded under the adult crane's wings, head and tail. There is a layer of four sheets of paper at these areas. Very thin and strong washi is a must.

Note:

Although the baby cranes are folded first, be sure to mark creases on the adult crane before folding baby cranes. Leave ample space at the connections—a little more than usual—but trim them smaller when folding is finished. For presentation, do not open the wings too much. Let the tail remain low and allow the model to stand on the baby cranes. This way it looks like a beautiful orchid blowing in the wind, as the title suggests.

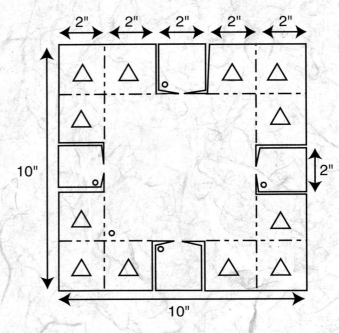

31. Myo Myo... Wonderful! Wonderful!

This is very similar to #12 Murakumo. Study the drawing to see the difference. Take extra care in folding the baby crane; it is very easy to tear.

Note:

The baby crane is folded first, but be sure to mark all the creases—including the adult crane's—before beginning to fold.

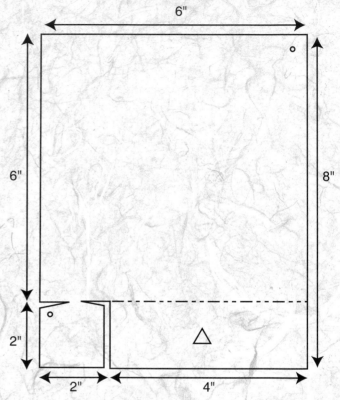

32. Hanabishi... A Diamond Shaped Flower

Here we have baby cranes sitting on top of an adult crane. A very cute model, this is very different in the way the adult crane's square is put together. #49 Hourai and #50 Karyobin are done in a similar manner.

Note:

Each baby crane is connected at each corner. Be sure to mark all the heads and fold the baby cranes first. All the folding lines starting at the connections of the baby cranes require the Mountain Fold, but the other folding lines require the Valley Fold. By folding these creases, a small eight-inch square is made out of the twelve-inch square. This eight-inch square becomes the adult crane.

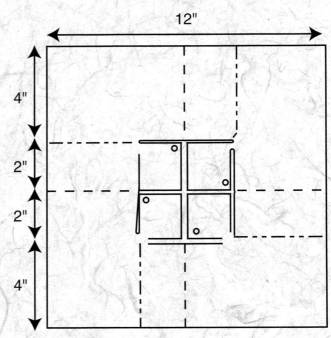

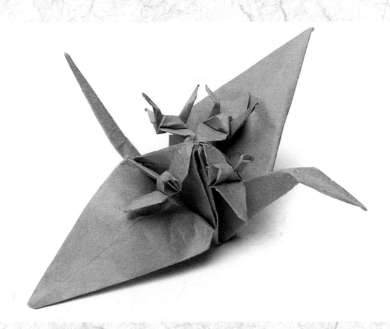

33. Ari no Toh... Ants' Tower

A model whre a baby crane sits on top of the adult crane's head. The method of folding is very interesting.

Note:

A, B, and C are folding lines. In order to see them clearly, draw them lightly on the paper except on the little square. This will be folded as a baby crane. Folding line C is a Valley Fold. Folding line A meets B to become the head of the adult crane. The adult crane is an eight-inch square, and the baby crane is a two-inch square.

Be sure to make all the creases before folding. Since the adult crane is made from a Blintz Fold, fairly thin washi is a must.

When presenting the work, be sure to have the tail set low. It looks better.

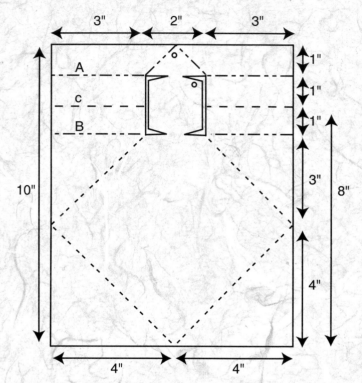

34. Yadorigi... Mistletoe

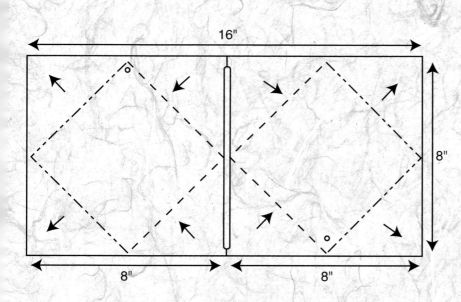

Two cranes are connected back to back in this model.

Note:

Corners A and B are blintz folded out in the direction of the arrow, and corners C and D are folded under in the direction of the arrow. As usual, make all the creases before folding. Be sure to mark the crane heads clearly.

35. Mittsu ga Ichi... Three-in-One

A beautiful model that is very unique and appealing. In the drawing, it is apparent that the wings of the adult cranes are broken. One of the wings of each crane is hidden under the baby crane and it is difficult to see. Actually, it is not there. Since the Blintz Fold is used, the paper should be fairly thin.

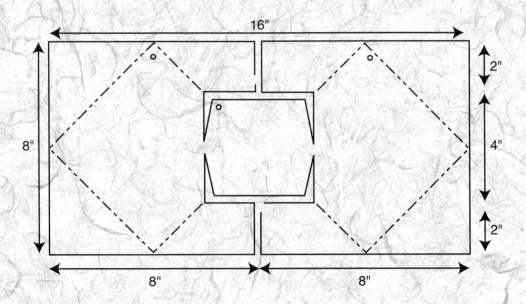

Note:
Make all creases before folding, and start to fold from the baby crane. All the heads face the same direction.

36. Aioi... Chasing Love

The drawing looks simple, but this is a very difficult model to fold since two cranes are connected at both their wings and heads. In each crane, one wing is made of only one sheet of paper while the other is made out of three layers of paper. The finished piece is very unique.

Note:

The diagonal creases are to be folded with the Valley Fold, but the horizontal/vertical fold creases use the Mountain Fold.

Fold A and B under C to make a three-layered wing. Be sure to make the head marks bigger than usual; otherwise it is difficult to see. Don't forget to make all the creases before folding.

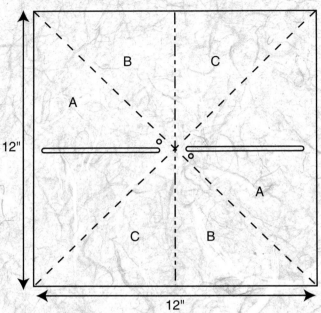

37. Omodaka... Flower Crest

A beautiful model that is somewhat difficult, since three cranes are connected to look like a flower.

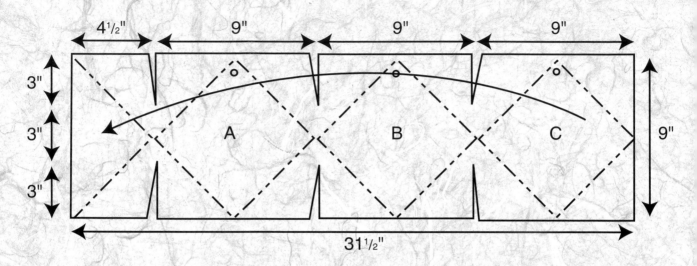

Note:

Fold in the order shown on the drawing. Each incision should be three inches deep. The top triangle piece is to be folded into the third crane to make a circle. Since the total work is done with Blintz Fold, a fairly thin washi should be used.

38. Sugomori... Cradle Nest

This model is made just like the top two cranes of #50 Karyobin, the most difficult to fold. The square of the adult crane is made by folding the diagonal lines to form a smaller square from the original square paper.

Note:

The baby crane is made up of a three-inch square which is 1/3 of the adult crane size. The length from the corner of the baby crane to its connecting point is measured from the corner of the large square to make a parallel creasing line. This is folded to make a smaller square for an adult crane. A thin washi is recommended due to the increased layers of paper.

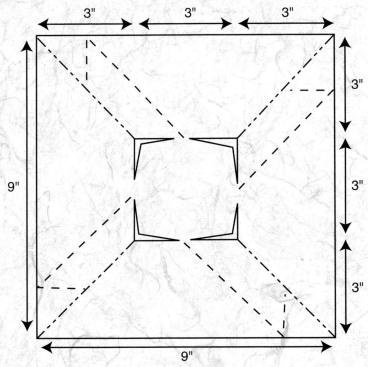

39. Yume no Kayoiji... The Passage to a Dream

With this interesting name, the model is both unique and inventive. Rokoan seems to like this pattern, and he keeps repeating it. #44 Sohji uses the exact same pattern.

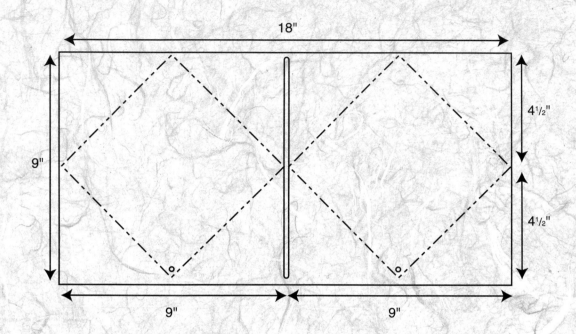

Note:
Two cranes are connected at their stomachs.

40. Tsukubane... A Shuttle Cock

The basic idea of this model is the same as #38 Sugomori; however, here there are two baby cranes on top of the adult crane.

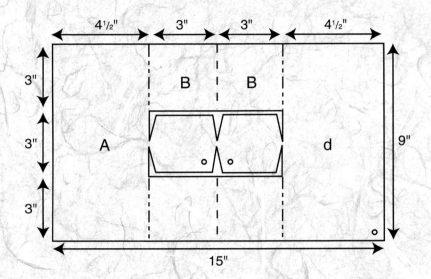

Note:

Fold the two baby cranes first. B is folded under A to make a nine inch square for the adult crane. Don't forget to make all the crease marks before folding.

41. Rindo Kuruma... A Blue Gentian

The drawing looks very simple, but it is not easy to fold. The cut at the center should be 2/3 into each square lengthwise. In the sample drawing, the square for the crane is a five-inch square; therefore, you cut three inches.

Note:

As usual, make all the creases before folding. Mark the crane heads clearly. All the heads are facing the center and the tails are pointing outward.

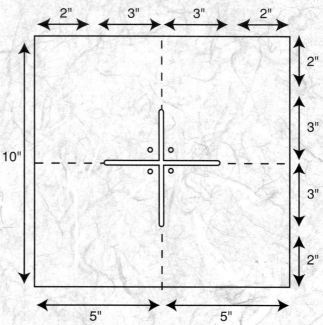

42. Uri no Tsuru... Vine of a Melon

According to the original book, two baby cranes are sitting side-by-side under the adult crane, and all cranes require the Blintz Fold. It is very difficult to fold because the baby cranes are hidden under the adult crane's Blintz Fold.

Note:

Be sure all the creases are marked before folding. Fold the baby cranes first. We advise that all the crane heads be marked on both sides of the paper.

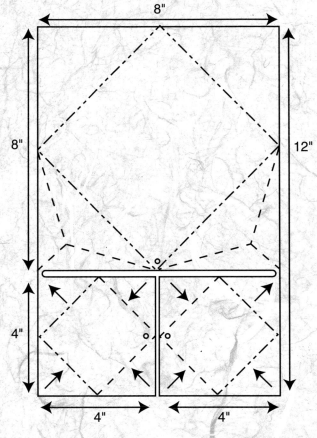

43. Hyakutsuru (Hyakkaku)... One Hundred Cranes

In this model 97 cranes are folded out of one sheet of paper! 96 baby cranes and one adult crane are folded from a square that is big enough for four baby cranes. That is why this is called 100 cranes. All the cranes are connected at one, two, three or four points. It is very difficult to fold, and much patience is required. There may be other models that are more difficult in technique, but this

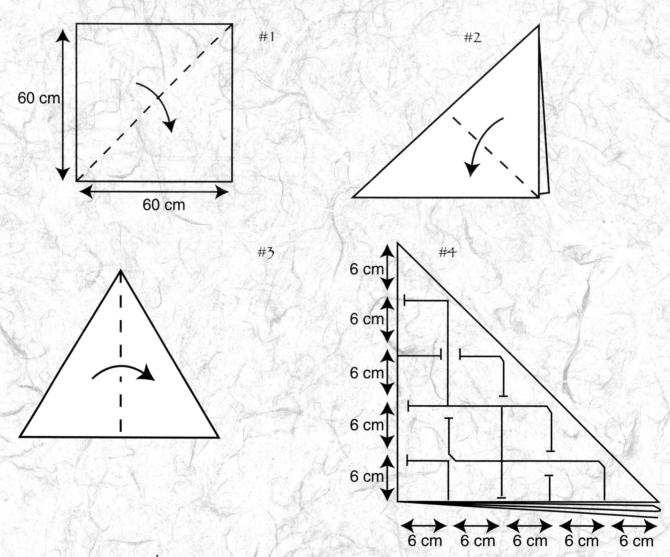

one requires time and patience.

Note:
Use the biggest square you can make out of a sheet of regular washi, 60cm x 60cm

1, #2, and #3 Fold in the order of the drawings.

#4:   Mark the 6cm x 6cm squares.

Note:

#5: Make all the cuts. Take extra care when cutting. Because of the size of washi, the drawing is done in centimeters. It is easier to divide the paper this way.

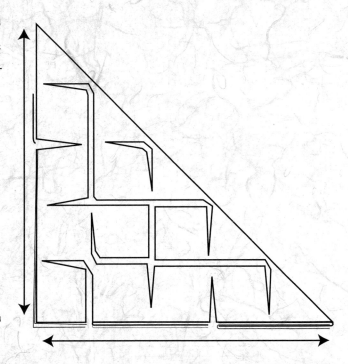

#6: After all the cuts are made, unfold and open the paper carefully.

#7: Mark all the crane heads.

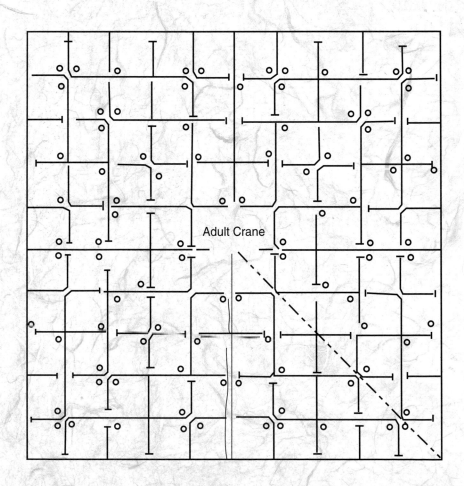

Adult Crane

#8: One quarter of the whole paper looks like this when folded.

#8

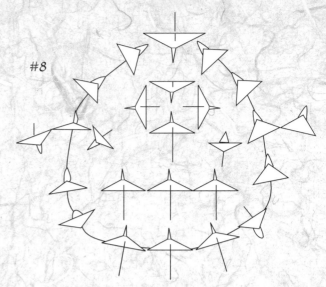

Note:

You can use washi which is thin and takes the creases easily such as Itajime and Chririzome.

Areas A, B, C, D each have 24 baby cranes. The adult crane is in the middle, occupying the square space for four baby cranes.

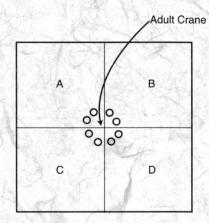

Adult Crane

A	B
C	D

28

44. Sohji... A Wise Man

This piece has cranes connected from one crane's back to another's stomach. The drawing/pattern is same as #34 Yadorigi, but the finished piece is quite different.

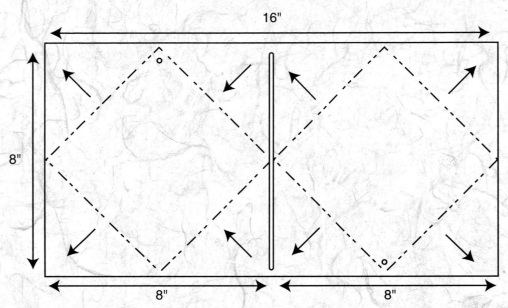

Note:

Start folding from A.

45. Hanatachibana... Flower of a Mandarin Orange

Here the cranes are connected from one tail to another's. It is quite difficult. Pay careful attention to avoid wrinkles. Again the pattern/drawing is the same as #34 Yadorigi, but the finished piece is very different. Each cut should be about 1/3 of the length for easier folding.

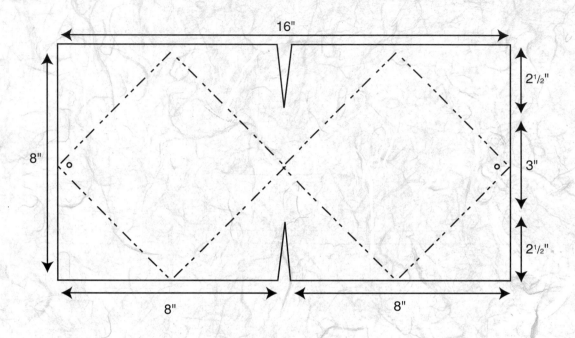

46. Hiyoku... Two Bodies Becoming One

Hiyoku is exactly the same as #37 Omodaka except that it has one less crane. There are only two cranes, not three, but it is more difficult to fold. Be sure to use strong, thin washi.

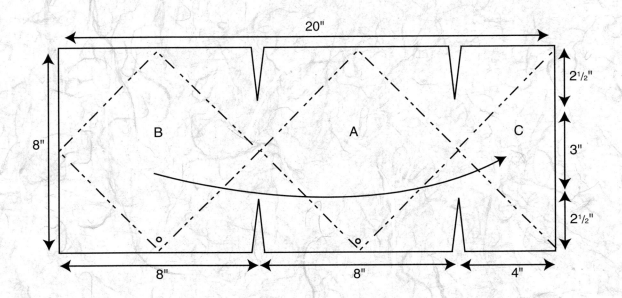

Note:

After folding A, match B and C to fold one crane. Each cut should be about 1/3 of the length for easier folding.

47. Hyotan-Machi... Town of Gourds

The drawing is the same as #41 Rindo Kuruma, but the wings are separated so that the finished piece looks a little different.

Note:

Leave ample space at the connections—more than the usual amount.

By adjusting the wings right and left, an interesting shape can be created for the finished piece.

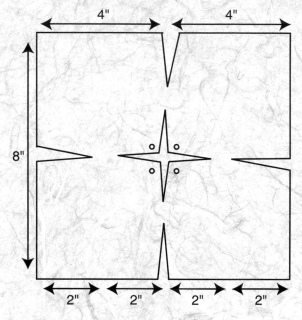

48. Sekirei... A Wagtail

A very different and difficult way of connecting two cranes. B is put through the hole in A before folding the cranes. Both cranes are made of blintz-folded squares.

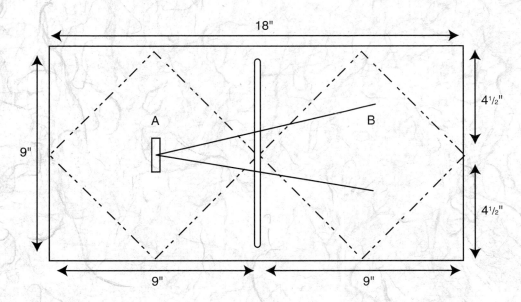

Note:

The hole in A should be approximately 1/4 inch x 1" in the center of the square.

After making a Blintz Fold, roll B into a one-inch diameter and squeeze it through the hole. Use a pencil to roll B.

Fold B first. A is very difficult to fold. Make every effort to avoid wrinkles.

49. Hourai... Island of Eternity

Very different from the others, each square at the four corners is made by layering the paper at each corner.

Note:

Dotted lines serve as the guide for layering. Be sure the squares for four cranes are perfectly square. There will be a pleat from layering on the wings of the four cranes.

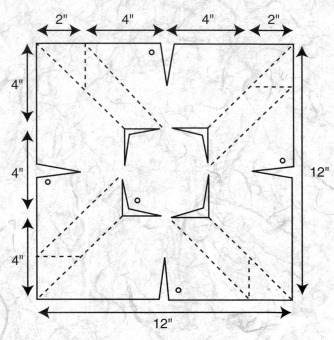

50. Karyobin... Phoenix

This is the most difficult model of all the Rokoan Style Origami. The utmost skill is required because five cranes are being folded, one on top of another. Since several layers of paper will be folded the right washi—thin and strong like Mino-gami or Chiri-zome—is best suited for this model. Again, metric measurement is used because it is easier to divide this way.

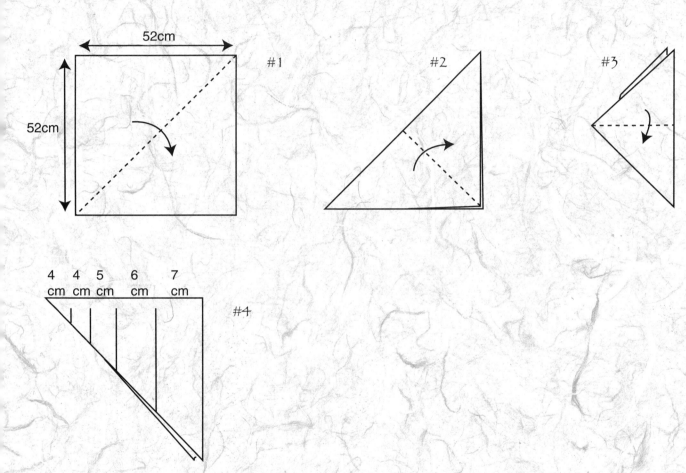

Note:

1. Use a 52cm x 52cm square paper. Fold it following the diagrams #1, #2, #3 and #4. Then cut at 4-4-5-6-7 ratio intervals. These cuttings should be at right angles to the fold. Leave uncut approximately 5mm from the fold.

2.   This model is folded like #38 Sugomori, but this has five layers of cranes. Be sure all the squares are perfect right-angle squares.

3.   Fold from the center crane.

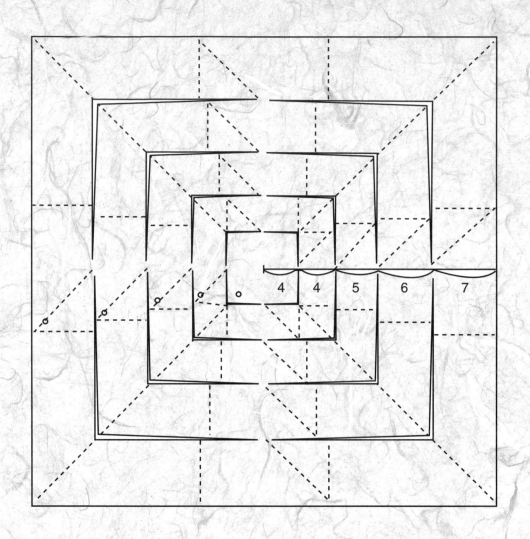

4 4 5 6 7

51. Tsuru-Furin... Crane Wind Chimes

Created by Masako Sakai

This is the very first model that Masako Sakai created based on Rokoan Style Origami. Under the center crane, cranes are connected to its wings, tail and stomach like the bells of a Furin (a wind chime). The center crane is folded from of three layers of paper.

Note:

1. Fold B under A. Cut C off. Fold the center crane first.

2. Two cranes made out of the Blintz Fold are connected to the stomach of the center crane. Leave enough space at these connections, for they tend to tear easily.

3. Now fold the clusters of three cranes. Then roll the corners of the remaining squares to make them look like the strings that hold bells in a Furin.

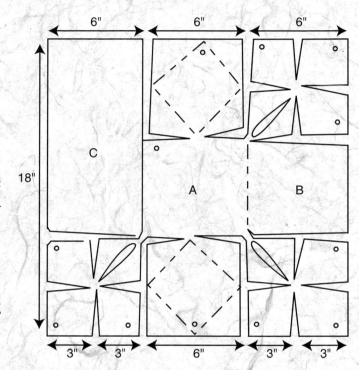

Part 3

More on Presentation

Now that you have folded all the creations by Rokoan, I suggest that you preserve the works, especially the complex ones like Hyakutsuru and Karyobin. Showcase your achievements since you might not make them again for a while. I feel that the best way to preserve Karyobin is to display it in a doll case. I've displayed Hyakutsuru in several different ways. It can be mounted on a canvas with an attractive and complementary Yuzenshi background. Uniform designs out of Yuzenshi can be cut to make it look like lace. Hyakutsuru made with a solid color washi looks great with this kind of background. Another way to display it is to cover a natural wood stump with Hyakutsuru. It looks like a flock of birds sitting on a rock.

The finished works may be used for interior decoration. A candle holder or the frame of a mirror may be decorated. Some panels of a shoji screen can be replaced with connected cranes. All are beautiful. Canvas-mounted works with plexiglas frames are always excellent.

Rokoan's original book ***Senbatsuru Orikata*** (***Folding a Thousand Cranes***), thought to be the oldest origami book, was published in 1797. Recently we received some very interesting information from the famous Japanese origamist, Kunihiko Kasahara. He told us that there is evidence that origami such as cranes, *yakko* (*court jester*), and boats existed 60 years prior to Rokoan's book. In 1993, commemorating its 20th Anniversary, the Japan Origami Society published a book called ***Origami in Classics*** by Tomo Takagi. This book mentions another publication called ***Ranma Zushiki*** (***Transom Design Diagrams***) published in 1734, in which origami is featured in decorative designs for a transom—not just simple origami models, but sophisticated ones like cranes, *yakko* (court jester), boats, komuso (Zen priest) and even unit/modular origami. Mr. Kasahara was excited because someone created intricate 24-sided modular origami over two centuries ago. Apparently there are several copies of this book still in existence.

I am hopeful that Rokoan's other book, ***Sounkaku*** (***Fundamental Cranes in the Cloud***), might be found some day. Perhaps it is gathering dust in a bookcase inside an old house. If it is found, we will be able to see what developed after this book or what preceded it in Rokoan's mind. Until then, let's enjoy creating these connected cranes and making them a part of our everyday life!

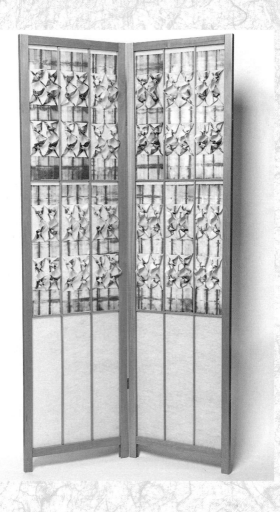